Daughters of Grace

THE WOMEN OF THE BIBLE
and THE GOD OF GRACE

by KRISTIN SCHMUCKER

www.thedailygraceco.com

Study Suggestions

Thank you for choosing this study to help you dig into God's Word. We are so passionate about women getting into Scripture, and we are praying that this study will be a tool to help you do that. Here are a few tips to help you get the most from this study:

• Before you begin, take time to look into the context of the book. Find out who wrote it and learn about the cultural climate it was written in, as well as where it fits on the biblical timeline. Then take time to read through the entire book of the Bible we are studying if you are able. This will help you to get the big picture of the book and will aid in comprehension, interpretation, and application.

• Start your study time with prayer. Ask God to help you understand what you are reading and allow it to transform you (Psalm 119:18).

• Look into the context of the book as well as the specific passage.

• Before reading what is written in the study, read the assigned passage! Repetitive reading is one of the best ways to study God's Word. Read it several times, if you are able, before going on to the study. Read in several translations if you find it helpful.

• As you read the text, mark down observations and questions. Write down things that stand out to you, things that you notice, or things that you don't understand. Look up important words in a dictionary or interlinear Bible.

• Look for things like verbs, commands, and references to God. Notice key terms and themes throughout the passage.

• After you have worked through the text, read what is written in the study. Take time to look up any cross-references mentioned as you study.

• Then work through the questions provided in the book. Read and answer them prayerfully.

• Paraphrase or summarize the passage, or even just one verse from the passage. Putting it into your own words helps you to slow down and think through every word.

• Focus your heart on the character of God that you have seen in this passage. What do you learn about God from the passage you have studied? Adore Him and praise Him for who He is

• Think and pray through application and how this passage should change you. Get specific with yourself. Resist the urge to apply the passage to others. Do you have sin to confess? How should this passage impact your attitude toward people or circumstances? Does the passage command you to do something? Do you need to trust Him for something in your life? How does the truth of the gospel impact your everyday life?

We recommend you have a Bible, pen, highlighters, and journal as you work through this study. We recommend that ball point pens instead of gel pens be used in the study book to prevent smearing. Here are several other optional resources that you may find helpful as you study:

• www.blueletterbible.org This free website is a great resource for digging deeper. You can find translation comparison, an interlinear option to look at words in the original languages, Bible dictionaries, and even commentary.

• A Dictionary. If looking up words in the Hebrew and Greek feels intimidating, look up words in English. Often times we assume we know the meaning of a word, but looking it up and seeing its definition can help us understand a passage better.

• A double spaced copy of the text. You can use a website like www.biblegateway.com to copy the text of a passage and print out a double spaced copy to be able to mark on easily. Circle, underline, highlight, draw arrows, and mark in any way you would like to help you dig deeper and work through a passage.

Introduction

Throughout the Old and New Testaments, we are introduced to a variety of women who had a significant impact on the story of redemption found in the Bible. Women from different social classes, nationalities, ages, and backgrounds had a profound influence in the events that unfold in Scripture. We see widows and orphans, old women and young girls live out the calling that God had given them. Throughout each woman's story, God's steadfast love and constant grace are evidenced.

Though written in a time when women were seen as secondary in society, the Bible shows great honor and respect to women. Women play very significant roles in a great number of biblical narratives. From the creation story, to the lives of the patriarchs, to the heads of government, the Old Testament shows women who served their families and their nation with remarkable bravery. The New Testament shows women as followers of Jesus every bit as passionate as the disciples and apostles. In fact, it is to a woman, the Samaritan woman at the well, that Jesus first revealed that He was the Messiah. And it was to another woman, Mary Magdalene, who after the resurrection Jesus would first reveal Himself to. The Bible defied the culture of the day by elevating and honoring women.

These women are like you and me. Their lives are a mixture of deep faith in a sovereign and loving God and the doubt and worry that comes so naturally to us as humans. Their lives are marked by their love for their Savior and the grace that only He can give.

These women are daughters of grace.

Eve

Eve

GENESIS 1-4

Eve is likely one of the most well-known women in the entire Bible. She was the first woman, and she is the mother of all. She was beautifully created from the rib of Adam and set in the garden with him with no shame and no sin. But it wasn't long before the wicked serpent came, and she was deceived into disobeying the command given by the Lord. The serpent did what Satan so often does and tried to get her to question the goodness of God and His Word. He tries to make Eve wonder if God truly wants the best for her or if there is something that she is missing. It is as though the story of Scripture has had this great and glorious beginning, and just a few chapters in we are filled with devastation as paradise has been ruined.

The fall has taken place, and a curse ensues. It is in the very words from God that describe the curse of sin and death that life, hope, and the gospel are presented for the first time in Scripture. In Genesis 3:15, the curse is set before us and the *protoevangelium* is given. The *protoevangelium* literally means "the first gospel," therefore, it is the first mention of the gospel in Scripture. The curse of God's judgment is given, but not without hope. There would be hope, and it would come through the woman that had set this whole curse in motion. Though Eve had sinned against the loving God and there would be consequences to the broken paradise, it would be through her own descendants that someday the curse would be forever broken and paradise would be restored. Even God's judgment was full of mercy and grace. The deliverer would come through Eve, and she would hold on to that promise for her entire life.

As children of God who are also created in His image and living in a fallen world, we can also cling to that promise. At the cross, Jesus crushed Satan, sin, and death with him. We have experienced firsthand the redemption that Eve hoped for, and now we can look forward to the day when death and sin will be forever defeated.

Eve's life reminds us that God redeems even our mistakes for His glory and for our good. The enemy may try to convince us that there is something better or something that we are missing out on, but we can trust in the Lord and in His Word. Though Eve set the curse in motion because of her own failure, she also was the first to receive the promise of the one that would set us all free. Our sin may be great, but His grace is so much greater.

WHAT DO WE LEARN ABOUT GOD AND
HIS CHARACTER IN THE LIFE OF EVE?

that even though she sinned
god still forgave her

WHAT CHARACTER QUALITIES,
POSITIVE OR NEGATIVE, DO WE SEE
DEMONSTRATED IN EVE'S LIFE?

that no one is perfect
and senless except god

WHAT CAN I LEARN FROM EVE'S STORY
THAT I CAN APPLY TO MY OWN LIFE?

that even if I sin
+ I repent god still loves
me and wants me to
follow him and seek
him in prayr and
Bible and to Centore
my Journey

Sarah

Sarah

GENESIS 12-23

Though Eve is remembered as the mother of all living, Sarah is remembered as the mother of the nation of Israel. As the wife to Abraham, her life is quite the adventure. When we meet Sarah in Scripture, she is already 65 years old and setting out on the adventure of a lifetime with her husband Abraham. We are immediately introduced to several things about her. We learn that even at the age of 65, she is a stunningly beautiful woman. We also learn that she has never borne a child.

Throughout the biblical account of Sarah, we see that her greatest desire was to have a child. It was a dream that already seemed impossible to her by the time we meet her. Her desire for children ate away at her. It was the thorn in her side, and every time we see strife in Sarah's life it comes back to her desire for a child. Her heart was broken, and she felt that God Himself must have been keeping her from bearing children (Genesis 16:2). Sarah must have felt so confused as God promised to make a great nation out of her husband Abraham. The Lord made so many promises to him, and yet to Sarah it must have felt that all these promises that the Lord had made depended on her ability or inability to bear a child for Abraham. She had laid this responsibility on herself, and the weight must have weighed heavy on her heart as the days, months, and years passed without a child.

Sarah felt that the promise of God was dependent on something she had to do, but she would eventually learn that God's promise was completely dependent on Him. God had promised the miraculous, and He would bring it to pass.

It was her desire to bring about God's promises on her own terms that led to one of Sarah's greatest downfalls — a plot for her husband to have a son through her servant. This was certainly not God's plan, and it was one that would haunt Sarah for years to come.

Yet the beauty of Sarah's story is this: Despite the strife her desire for a child sometimes caused and her impatience as she waited for God to fulfill the promise He had made, the book of Hebrews tells us that through it all Sarah held on to hope and believed that the "the one who had promised was faithful" (Hebrews 11:11). She was utterly human, and yet in her heart she believed the promise that God had made to Abraham and to her. For that reason, she is listed in Hebrews 11 among the great heroes of the faith. She was at times frustrated with waiting and even tried to do things in her own strength. Yet in the end, she placed her faith in the Almighty God, and He did bring to pass the promise that He had made. At the age of 90, she bore a son. God had done what He had said He would do (Genesis 21:1).

Sarah's life reminds us that we do not have to earn God's favor. We already have it, and He always keeps His promises. He will be faithful. God was faithful to Sarah, and we can be sure that He will be faithful to us.

WHAT DO WE LEARN ABOUT GOD AND HIS CHARACTER IN THE LIFE OF SARAH?

that god made a promise, and fulfed it in his time, not Sarahs

WHAT CHARACTER QUALITIES, POSITIVE OR NEGATIVE, DO WE SEE DEMONSTRATED IN SARAH'S LIFE?

that even though she was Impatient she kept her faith in god to keep his promise

WHAT CAN I LEARN FROM SARAH'S STORY THAT I CAN APPLY TO MY OWN LIFE?

To have more patence, And to wat on gods time and keep my faith And keep praying and thanking god for all his love & what he provides for me & my family

Amen

Hagar

Hagar

GENESIS 16, 21

When we think of biblical heroines, Hagar does not usually make the list. She was a servant of Abraham and Sarah, a foreigner, and a woman in distress; but we also see that she was a woman seen by the Lord.

Hagar was caught in a mess that was not her choice. Her mistress Sarah, who had not had any children, concocted a plan to do things her own way and provide her husband an heir through her servant Hagar. As a servant, Hagar had no choice in the matter. Abraham listened to Sarah. Hagar became a wife to Abraham, and soon she became pregnant. Sarah dealt harshly with Hagar, and we see a pregnant and likely very scared Hagar flee into the wilderness. It is in the wilderness that Hagar is met by the angel of the Lord. This was likely a *theophany*. A theophany is an appearance of God Himself speaking to Hagar that day. This seems evident because He speaks in first person as the Lord. He encourages her to return to Abraham and Sarah but makes her a promise. Abraham had been promised a great nation, and now we see this servant girl promised that her offspring would be multiplied. The Lord tells her to name her son Ishmael because God had heard her. Hagar then calls the Lord a unique name, El Roi—meaning the God who sees. Hagar recognized that the Lord saw her right where she was. He saw the mess that she was in, and He cared enough to come to her.

Later in her story, Sarah asks Hagar to leave and take Ishmael. In desperation, while in the wilderness with her son near death, the Lord appears to her again. He provides her water in the desert and hope for her weary soul. Surely her life had not turned out the way that she had planned, but He is the God who sees. He had seen her every step of the way and provided for her and her son through it all.

Perhaps your life has not turned out the way that you had planned either. Perhaps the circumstances of life, whether caused by yourself or someone else, have left you feeling desperate and alone. There is hope. Our God is the God who sees. He hears your burdens, and He sees you right where you are. He is good, and He is faithful. He will provide water in the wilderness and hope for your soul.

"Our God is the God who sees."

WHAT DO WE LEARN ABOUT GOD AND HIS CHARACTER IN THE LIFE OF HAGAR?

That he never left her, no matter how bad things happend

WHAT CHARACTER QUALITIES, POSITIVE OR NEGATIVE, DO WE SEE DEMONSTRATED IN HAGAR'S LIFE?

that she prsevered even though she was unaatan she kept faith & prayd still seeking god

WHAT CAN I LEARN FROM HAGAR'S STORY THAT I CAN APPLY TO MY OWN LIFE?

never give up, no matter how bad things get. to keep my faith And keep Seeking the lord & pray!!..

Rebekah

Rebekah
GENESIS 24-28

Rebekah's story is one mixed with tremendous faith and doubt in God's plan. We meet her as the young woman at the well who is willing to help a stranger. As she draws water for him and his camels, she does not realize that she is forever changing the course of her life. It took great faith for her to leave her family and follow this man to a faraway land and marry a man that she did not know. She would marry Isaac and be welcomed into God's grand plan for the nation of Israel.

It would be many years before Rebekah would have a child, but God would eventually bless her with twins that would wrestle in her womb. It was her children that would cause her to doubt the Lord's plan and to try to do things in her own way. She would play a pivotal role in having Esau sell his birthright to her younger son, Jacob, who then claims the birthright and blessing of Isaac. These events would lead to Jacob fleeing his home. Instead of trusting the Lord, Rebekah did things her own way, and the consequences included her beloved son being far from her for the rest of her life. The consequences of the rift between her sons would also have long-lasting effects as they would be nations at odds for centuries. The nations would be set against each other even during the time of Christ when Herod, a descendant of Esau, would seek to kill the young Jesus, a descendant of Jacob.

And yet, through it all, we can see how God used Rebekah. She would be an important matriarch in the lineage of Israel. Though she was an imperfect woman with faith that sometimes waivered, she was used by the God who had called her out of her father's house and into the beautiful adventure that He had set before her.

Her life reminds us that God uses imperfect women to fulfill His plan. Rebekah made mistakes and tried to do things her own way. She struggled to trust that God's plan was really what would be best for her and her family, and yet God used her. We are imperfect women, and yet God in His rich love and mercy will use us as well.

"God uses imperfect women to fulfill His plan."

WHAT DO WE LEARN ABOUT GOD AND HIS
CHARACTER IN THE LIFE OF REBEKAH?

that she loved her in
all her flaws

WHAT CHARACTER QUALITIES,
POSITIVE OR NEGATIVE, DO WE SEE
DEMONSTRATED IN REBEKAH'S LIFE?

her love for her Children

WHAT CAN I LEARN FROM REBEKAH'S
STORY THAT I CAN APPLY TO MY OWN
LIFE?

that Sometimes our plans
do not turn out in our
favor, but to keep
trusting god in Everything

Rachel

Rachel

GENESIS 29-35

Rachel is known for her beauty and for the way that Jacob desperately loved her. But beauty and love were not enough to make her happy. Jacob would labor seven years to win her as his bride, but a trick from her father left him to wake up to Rachel's older sister the day after the wedding. We often focus on Jacob in this portion of the story as he was tricked by Laban into marrying a woman that he had not intended to marry; but imagine the anguish Rachel felt as she was forced by her father, at the last moment, to not participate in what would have been her own wedding. Instead, she watched her sister marry the man that she loved.

Jacob would work for seven more years to marry Rachel, and eventually they would be together. Even though they eventually would marry, Jacob's loyalty was divided between two sisters. Two sisters would chase after his favor; it was of no fault of their own that they found themselves in this position.

Rachel was loved and she was beautiful, but she was also childless. While her sister bore children to her beloved husband, she had none. Envy of her sister stirred in her heart. Rachel felt bitter and forgotten. Her life had certainly not turned out the way that she had planned. Her romantic fairy tales had come crashing down. Her desire for children would cause strife between her, her sister, and her husband, and she was left feeling worthless and alone.

But God remembered Rachel (Genesis 30:22). When she felt forgotten and alone, she was seen by the Lord. She would bear two sons, Joseph and Benjamin, and God would use her children in His perfect plan. Her life may not have turned out the way that she had planned, but God would redeem her story.

God will use your story as well, even if life has not turned out the way that you planned. Even if you feel alone and rejected, He sees you. He remembers you. His plan for you is good.

"Even if you feel alone and rejected, He sees you."

WHAT DO WE LEARN ABOUT GOD AND HIS CHARACTER IN THE LIFE OF RACHEL?

that he never left her or forget about her

WHAT CHARACTER QUALITIES, POSITIVE OR NEGATIVE, DO WE SEE DEMONSTRATED IN RACHEL'S LIFE?

that she kept praying d waiting

WHAT CAN I LEARN FROM RACHEL'S STORY THAT I CAN APPLY TO MY OWN LIFE?

Do not give up, And wait on gods time

He is Never late!

NOW WITHOUT FAITH IT IS IMPOSSIBLE TO PLEASE GOD, SINCE THE ONE WHO DRAWS NEAR TO HIM MUST BELIEVE THAT HE EXISTS AND THAT HE REWARDS THOSE WHO SEEK HIM.

Hebrews 11:6

WHICH WOMAN STUCK OUT TO YOU MOST THIS WEEK AND WHY?

WHAT DID YOU OBSERVE FROM THIS WEEK'S READING
ABOUT GOD AND HIS CHARACTER?

WHAT DOES THIS WEEK'S READING TEACH ABOUT THE
CONDITION OF MANKIND AND ABOUT YOURSELF?

HOW DOES THIS WEEK'S READING POINT TO THE GOSPEL?

HOW SHOULD YOU RESPOND TO THIS WEEK'S READING?
WHAT IS THE PERSONAL APPLICATION?

WHAT SPECIFIC ACTION STEPS CAN YOU TAKE
TO APPLY THIS WEEK'S READING?

Leah

Leah
GENESIS 29-35

Both Rachel and her sister Leah had been thrust into a life that was not what they had planned. Leah was the older sister. In this culture, it was customary that she would marry first. But she was not the stunning beauty that her sister was, which certainly she was aware of. Jacob had worked seven years for her sister; but on the eve of the wedding, Leah's father hatched a plan that Leah would marry Jacob in disguise. When the wedding was over and morning came, Jacob realized he had been tricked and Leah was now married to a man that never wanted her.

But the Lord saw her. He did not see her as the unwanted bride or rejected one, but as his own beloved child. And despite the rejection that she lived with from her husband, we see that she praised the Lord with her life (Genesis 29:35). The Lord would bless her with many children, and she knew that even though she was rejected by her husband, her children were a gift from the Lord. And though she was not the most beautiful sister, or the chosen bride, it was through her that King David, and someday Jesus the Messiah, would come. Jacob may not have chosen her, but God certainly had. He chose her to be an important mother in the line of Jesus.

Though her life may have been filled with longing for a husband who would always love another woman, God gave Leah a purpose far greater than she could have ever dreamed. Certainly there have been times that we have all felt like Leah — times when we compared our life to someone else, times when we felt rejected, and times we felt that we never measured up. But God has a purpose for each of us. He has uniquely created us to fulfill the role that He has made for us, and He sees us right where we are. We can praise Him because even if life is not exactly the way that we had planned, His plan is perfect.

"But the Lord saw her. He did not see her as the unwanted bride or rejected one, but as his own beloved child."

WHAT DO WE LEARN ABOUT GOD AND HIS
CHARACTER IN THE LIFE OF LEAH?

WHAT CHARACTER QUALITIES,
POSITIVE OR NEGATIVE, DO WE SEE
DEMONSTRATED IN LEAH'S LIFE?

WHAT CAN I LEARN FROM LEAH'S STORY
THAT I CAN APPLY TO MY OWN LIFE?

The Hebrew Midwives

The Hebrew Midwives
EXODUS 1

In the first chapter of Exodus, we meet five woman who bravely and fearlessly stood against the grain and helped deliver a nation. The first two that we meet are Shiphrah and Puah, who were two of the Hebrew midwives. Pharaoh was beginning to be fearful of the growing Hebrew nation and commanded the midwives to kill any son that was born to the Hebrew women. But the midwives feared God more than they feared man (Proverbs 9:10), and we are told that God dealt well with them because of it. They did not kill the male children, and because of their action God grew the nation of Israel. The deliverer of Israel would be born during a time when a handful of women decided to serve God instead of man.

Midwives at this time are believed by most scholars to have been barren women with no children of their own; but in verse 21 we learn that because of the midwives obedience to the Lord, God gave them families of their own. It must have taken great faith and bravery to obey the Lord and defy the king, but these women were women of purpose and integrity who were far more concerned about pleasing the Lord than with appeasing the Pharaoh. God would reward them greatly for their faith and obedience.

As women, we are often caught in a position where we must choose to please the Lord or to please man. We are often crippled with the desire to please others, but these midwives stand as a beautiful example of placing our trust in God alone. Let us be women who live lives that please the Lord and not just live to please those around us. Let us be women of valiant faith who know that our faith is what pleases the Lord, and that He will reward us for our trust in Him (Hebrews 11:6). Let us be women who serve the Lord no matter what.

"Let us be women who live lives that please the Lord and not just live to please those around us."

WHAT DO WE LEARN ABOUT GOD AND HIS CHARACTER IN THE LIVES OF THE HEBREW MIDWIVES?

WHAT CHARACTER QUALITIES, POSITIVE OR NEGATIVE, DO WE SEE DEMONSTRATED IN THE LIVES OF THE HEBREW MIWIVES?

WHAT CAN I LEARN FROM THE STORY OF THE HEBREW MIDWIVES THAT I CAN APPLY TO MY OWN LIFE?

The Mothers of Moses

The Mothers of Moses
EXODUS 2

Two women, who were worlds apart yet neighbors, would be used by God to raise one little boy to become the deliverer of His people. These two women had nothing in common except for a mother's love for the same baby boy.

Jochebed was the mother of Moses. She gave birth to him among the slaves' quarters in the land of Egypt, far from the land that had been promised to their people years before. Pharaoh had ordered all of the baby boys to be killed at birth, but just like the Hebrew midwives, she could not bear to kill this precious gift from God. She defied the king and kept him hidden for three months, but soon she couldn't hide him any longer and her heart was breaking. Hope must have seemed lost when she set him in a basket that she had made herself and placed him in the Nile River with his older sister, Miriam, watching all the way. But God had a plan for that baby boy of hers, and her bravery and courage set the plan in motion.

Down the river another young woman would see a basket while she was bathing in the Nile. While Pharaoh had ordered that this baby be killed, his own daughter would be the one to rescue Moses from the dangerous river and from her own people. She took pity on him and raised him as her own. To the delight of the woman on the other side of the river grieving her son, Pharaoh's daughter would send for her to nurse the boy and would even pay her to care for the son she loved.

God was working all along and preparing this young boy to deliver his own people. A hurting mother who felt desperate and alone and a princess who had compassion were both used by God to save the people of God.

There may be times that we feel alone and desperate, but we are never alone. He is there at every turn working His perfect plan. He uses imperfect women who will step up and do the right thing, even when they do not understand what the outcome may be. No matter what your situation in life, slave or princess, He will use you for His glory if you will let Him.

"He is there at every turn working His perfect plan."

WHAT DO WE LEARN ABOUT GOD
AND HIS CHARACTER IN THE LIVES
OF THE MOTHERS OF MOSES?

WHAT CHARACTER QUALITIES,
POSITIVE OR NEGATIVE, DO WE
SEE DEMONSTRATED IN THE LIVES
OF THE MOTHERS OF MOSES?

WHAT CAN I LEARN FROM THE STORY
OF THE MOTHERS OF MOSES THAT
I CAN APPLY TO MY OWN LIFE?

Rahab

Rahab

JOSHUA 2:1-21; 6:17-25; MATTHEW 1:5;
HEBREWS 11:31; JAMES 2:25

Rahab is another unlikely heroine of Scripture. We are introduced to her as Rahab the prostitute, but her faith would make her so much more than a woman defined only by her sin. She would be a woman defined by grace and redemption.

God used her to hide the two Hebrew spies as they came into the city of Jericho from the wicked king. Joshua 2:11 shows us her daring proclamation of faith in the one true God as she went against everything her people stood for. Rahab had heard about the God of Israel and all that He had done to rescue His people, and she placed her faith in God alone. God's steadfast love would be poured out on Rahab and her whole family. His magnificent grace and love would be so great to her that she would not even know its full extent during her life.

Just as God had said, the city was destroyed; but one woman and her family were rescued. Rahab was saved because of her great faith.

Rahab is mentioned several other places in Scripture. She is commended for her faith in James 2:25 and Hebrews 11:31, and she is honored as a woman that feared the Lord more than she feared men. But it is her position in the genealogy of Jesus that is such a beautiful picture of redemption (Matthew 1:5). God took a woman who was an outcast of society and made her an important part of the family tree of the Messiah.

Rahab is a picture of the extravagant grace of our Savior. Rahab was a woman despised even by her own wicked culture, and yet when she placed her faith in the one true God, her life and destiny were transformed. She is remembered now as a woman of great faith. She is defined by her Savior and not by her sin. God uses women who are flawed, but who will simply place their faith in Him. We are no longer defined by our sin; but instead, we are defined by the grace and redemption that is found in God alone. God used Rahab, and He will certainly use you.

"God uses women who are flawed, but who will simply place their faith in Him."

WHAT DO WE LEARN ABOUT GOD AND HIS
CHARACTER IN THE LIFE OF RAHAB?

WHAT CHARACTER QUALITIES,
POSITIVE OR NEGATIVE, DO WE SEE
DEMONSTRATED IN RAHAB'S LIFE?

WHAT CAN I LEARN FROM RAHAB'S STORY
THAT I CAN APPLY TO MY OWN LIFE?

Deborah

Deborah
JUDGES 4-5

Deborah stands out in Scripture. We are introduced to her as a wife, prophetess, and judge. She filled many roles and did them all with faithfulness to the Lord. Deborah would lead the people in battle, but more importantly she would lead their hearts back to the Lord.

Deborah comes on to the scene during a turbulent time in the history of the nation of Israel. The book of Judges tells over and over of the cycle of sin and obedience that the nation went through. They would obey and then they would slip back into doing what was right in their own eyes. Deborah becomes judge at a time when the people are doing what was right in their own eyes, but she would bring them back to the Lord. Deborah calls Barak to go up into battle, but he tells her that he will not go without her. Deborah was clearly a woman who was well-respected for her wisdom and insight from the Lord. Deborah did go with him and declared that God would deliver the evil Sisera into the hand of a woman. This was certainly scandalous for this time period, but it is just a reminder that God does things in His own way. He uses the most unlikely people to do His work and bring Him glory.

When the battle is won, we see the song of Deborah. Her beautiful song of praise to the Lord showed her deep love and devotion to God. She gave Him all the glory for the battle that had been won under her leadership. God had done a great thing, and the land and people were given rest as their hearts were turned back to Him under Deborah's leadership.

Deborah was a woman of courage and honor. She bravely did what God had called her to do and then praised Him for what He had accomplished through her. Her life reminds us that God can use us all, even when it seems like we are an unlikely choice. And when we are used by Him, we must not take the credit for ourselves, but instead realize that the victory is because of God working through us. What a joy to be used by the Lord.

"when we are used by Him, we must not take the credit for ourselves, but instead realize that the victory is because of God working through us."

"She gave Him all the glory for the battle that had been won under her leadership."

WHAT DO WE LEARN ABOUT GOD AND HIS
CHARACTER IN THE LIFE OF DEBORAH?

WHAT CHARACTER QUALITIES,
POSITIVE OR NEGATIVE, DO WE SEE
DEMONSTRATED IN DEBORAH'S LIFE?

WHAT CAN I LEARN FROM DEBORAH'S
STORY THAT I CAN APPLY TO
MY OWN LIFE?

TRUST IN HIM AT ALL TIMES,
YOU PEOPLE; POUR OUT YOUR
HEARTS BEFORE HIM. GOD
IS OUR REFUGE. *SELAH.*

Psalm 62:8

WEEK TWO
reflection

WHICH WOMAN STUCK OUT TO YOU MOST THIS WEEK AND WHY?

WHAT DID YOU OBSERVE FROM THIS WEEK'S READING
ABOUT GOD AND HIS CHARACTER?

WHAT DOES THIS WEEK'S READING TEACH ABOUT THE
CONDITION OF MANKIND AND ABOUT YOURSELF?

HOW DOES THIS WEEK'S READING POINT TO THE GOSPEL?

HOW SHOULD YOU RESPOND TO THIS WEEK'S READING?
WHAT IS THE PERSONAL APPLICATION?

WHAT SPECIFIC ACTION STEPS CAN YOU TAKE
TO APPLY THIS WEEK'S READING?

Jael

Jael
JUDGES 4-5

Right in the middle of the story of Deborah we meet Jael, another woman used by the Lord. Jael was a woman who displayed fearless courage and fulfilled the prophecy that Sisera would be delivered into the hands of a woman. Jael was that woman.

Sisera fled from the battle right to Jael's tent. It seems from Scripture that Jael's own husband had taken the side of the evil Sisera and Jabin, but Jael would stand alone for truth. Sisera asked for refuge in her tent, and she allowed him in. When he asked for a glass of water, she gave him some milk to drink and let him settle into a deep sleep. While the evil man slept, she took a tent peg and hammer and drove the peg through his temple. It is such a shocking story, and yet we must realize that this woman used what she had and defeated the evil enemy. The Lord had promised deliverance by a woman. Jael was that woman because she used what she knew and what she had right where she was.

Jael would be praised in Deborah's song as "blessed among women." In Deborah's song, we learn a bit more about Sisera. Sisera was an evil man who was expected by even his own mother to be out raping and disgracing women as the spoil of his victory. How ironic that it would be at the hand of a woman that he would be defeated. Even though Sisera objectified and mistreated women, it was a woman that would bring victory for the land of Israel and final defeat for Sisera.

Jael did what she could with what she had, and her life reminds us to do the same. It is easy to feel that we do not have all that we need to serve the Lord. It sometimes feels like there must be others who are more worthy and suitable to do what He has called us to do. And yet God will use us right where we are with the gifts and talents He has given us, because it is where He has placed us and called us to be. He only asks that we be surrendered to Him, and He is pleased when we serve Him right where we are.

"God will use us right where we are with the gifts and talents He has given us"

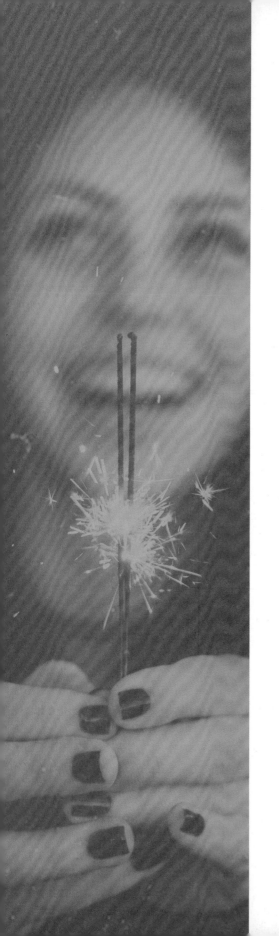

WHAT DO WE LEARN ABOUT GOD AND HIS
CHARACTER IN THE LIFE OF JAEL?

WHAT CHARACTER QUALITIES,
POSITIVE OR NEGATIVE, DO WE SEE
DEMONSTRATED IN JAEL'S LIFE?

WHAT CAN I LEARN FROM JAEL'S STORY
THAT I CAN APPLY TO MY OWN LIFE?

Ruth

Ruth

RUTH 1-4

The story of Ruth is one of the most compelling in Scripture. Perhaps it is because everyone loves a romance, and this is a great one. The account takes place during the time of the judges. It was a difficult and turbulent time for the nation of Israel. Yet, in the midst of the physical and spiritual famine that took place in the land, we see a story of redemption that points us to our own story of redemption.

It was during this great famine that Elimelech and Naomi fled Israel with their two sons to the pagan nation of Moab. Moab was not a place that Israelites would usually go, but I suppose that just shows us how dire the situation was. After years in Moab, tragedy strikes. Elimelech and his two sons all die. This left Naomi and her two daughter-in-laws, Ruth and Orpah, all alone. Naomi decides to return to her homeland and the two women decide to follow her. As they travel, Naomi pleads with the women to return to their own families. Orpah heads back, but Ruth will not leave Naomi alone and commits to go with her.

When they had returned to Bethlehem, Ruth goes out to glean in the fields of Boaz. As a poor young widow, this was a way for her to be provided with food that was left in the fields. It was a practice put into place to care for the less fortunate in Leviticus 19:9-10. When Ruth told Naomi that she had gleaned in the field of Boaz, Naomi identified Boaz as a close relative. The word here for close relative is *goel*, which means so much more than just a relative. The word implies redemption, deliverance, an avenger, and a kinsman redeemer. This person was meant to point to Jesus, who would be our Kinsman Redeemer. Naomi told Ruth to do something uncommon in that day. Ruth would be very forward and essentially propose marriage to Boaz when she identified him as her *goel*. Boaz was a man of great character, and he would be that kinsman redeemer. He put everything in order to ensure that he was the one and there was no other that would step up to be Ruth's redeemer.

We learn so much from this short story in the book of Ruth. We see that God uses ordinary people to fulfill His perfect will. Ruth was a Moabite, a foreign woman who, despite her lineage, put her trust in the God of Israel. Boaz was the direct descendant of another woman we have learned of, Rahab. As the son of a woman who had lived a sinful life and been redeemed from it, Boaz reminds us of all that God did for Rahab and her line. Boaz and Ruth would become the great

great grandparents of David and have an important role in the line of the Messiah.

In this story we also are reminded of our own Redeemer. John Macarthur points out that "Jesus is our true kinsman redeemer, who becomes our human brother, brings us back from our bondage to evil, redeems our lives from death, and ultimately returns to us everything we lost because of our sin." Jesus changes everything for us. We may have been outcasts from a foreign land like Ruth, but now we have become His chosen bride and are loved beyond measure by our Redeemer.

WHAT DO WE LEARN ABOUT GOD AND HIS CHARACTER IN THE LIFE OF RUTH?

WHAT CHARACTER QUALITIES, POSITIVE OR NEGATIVE, DO WE SEE DEMONSTRATED IN RUTH'S LIFE?

WHAT CAN I LEARN FROM RUTH'S STORY THAT I CAN APPLY TO MY OWN LIFE?

Hannah

Hannah
1 SAMUEL 1-2

We are introduced to Hannah at a time in the history of Israel when the nation was not focused on the Lord, and yet this young woman was. Hannah is the wife of Elkanah, and she was obviously very loved by him according to Scripture. But Hannah did not have any children, and Elkanah had another wife, likely for that very reason. Hannah so deeply desired a child. Her heart must have ached month after month as she was reminded of her infertility. Hannah could have become a bitter woman, and we probably would not have blamed her because of the heartache that she endured. Instead of living with bitterness, Hannah took her sorrow to the Lord. She poured out her heart to the Lord and promised Him that if she was given a son, she would give Him to the Lord for service all the days of his life.

Hannah came to the temple each year with her husband, and on one particular trip it seems that she stood out in the temple as she poured out her heart before the Lord in prayer. I Samuel 1:12 points out that she continued in prayer, and Hannah's life is certainly an example of persistent prayer. When it seemed she had nowhere else to turn, she continually turned to the Lord with the desires of her heart. In this time in Israel's history when they were not focused on the Lord, her fervent prayer must have stood out. Eli the priest even questioned her, concerned that she may be drunk. In a time when many did not pour out their heart to the Lord, Eli must have been shocked. He immediately answered that God would grant her petition. Hannah had brought her burden to the Lord that day and poured out every part of her heart, and now she had left her burden at His feet.

God did hear the prayer of Hannah, and I Samuel 1:19 tells us that God remembered her. When her son is born, the overflow of her heart is jubilant praise to the Lord. Hannah's beautiful prayer that is recorded in I Samuel 2 praises God for who He is, shows us the depth of Hannah's knowledge of the Lord, and reminds us of the Magnificat that Mary the mother of Jesus would some day write about her own Son. Hannah kept her vow, and when her son was weaned she took him to the temple where he would serve the Lord all the days of his life. It was a desperate time for the nation of Israel, and the desperate prayers of a young woman would give the nation the man that it needed to help bring the nation back to the Lord.

Hannah's life reminds us to pour our own hearts out to the Lord (Psalm 62:8, Psalm 142:1-3). She reminds us that God hears our prayer and that there is value in passionate and persistent prayer. No matter what life brings us, we can turn to the Lord and take our sorrows to Him. He does hear, and He will answer. And when He answers, let us be like Hannah, full of praise for who He is and all He has done.

WHAT DO WE LEARN ABOUT GOD AND HIS CHARACTER IN THE LIFE OF HANNAH?

WHAT CHARACTER QUALITIES, POSITIVE OR NEGATIVE, DO WE SEE DEMONSTRATED IN HANNAH'S LIFE?

WHAT CAN I LEARN FROM HANNAH'S STORY THAT I CAN APPLY TO MY OWN LIFE?

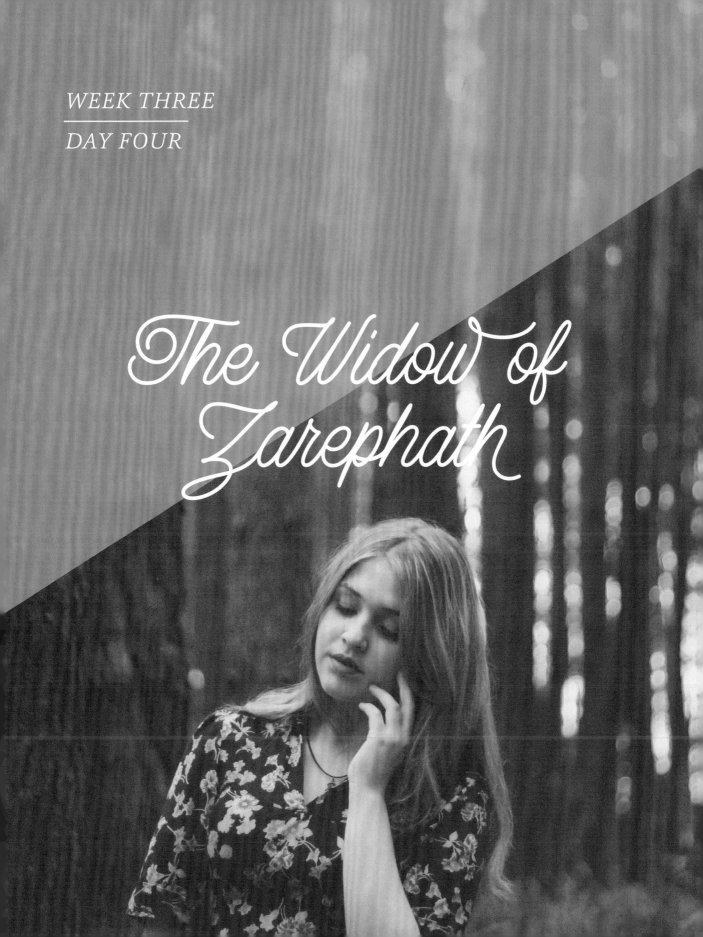

The Widow of Zarephath

The Widow of Zarephath

1 KINGS 17:8-24

We don't even know her name. We read of her in I Kings where she is just referred to as the widow of Zarephath. She is not an Israelite, but a foreign woman. Her husband has died, and she lives alone with her young son. We meet them when there is a famine in the land, and she has very little left to provide for herself and her young son. She must have been shocked when Elijah came and asked her for water and bread. She didn't have any bread, and she wasn't even sure that she had enough left for that night's dinner. She told Elijah that her plan was to cook what she had left for her and her son and then prepare to die. Elijah told her not to fear and to make her cake and a little for him as well. He told her that God had said that her jar of flour would never run out and her jug of oil would never run dry as long as there was famine in the land. She could have said no, but she may have felt like she had nothing to lose, so she did what he said.

Since she did what he said, they ate for many days. Just like the prophet had said, that little jar of flour and that little jug of oil never did run out. Each day when she went about her everyday duties, she was reminded again of the grace that she had been given. It was not the last time that she would see God work on her part. When her son became ill and died, the prophet would raise him from the dead. God was teaching this woman that He would provide for every need she would ever face. He would do what He had said that He would do.

He will do what He has promised us as well. He will be with us every day. He will never let us down. And every day when we are reminded again of His fresh mercy and grace for our day, we will also be reminded of His great love for us. He is always faithful.

"God was teaching this woman that He would provide for every need she would ever face. He would do what He had said that He would do."

WHAT DO WE LEARN ABOUT GOD
AND HIS CHARACTER IN THE LIFE
OF THE WIDOW OF ZAREPHATH?

WHAT CHARACTER QUALITIES,
POSITIVE OR NEGATIVE, DO WE
SEE DEMONSTRATED IN THE LIFE
OF THE WIDOW OF ZAREPHATH?

WHAT CAN I LEARN FROM THE STORY
OF THE WIDOW OF ZAREPHATH THAT
I CAN APPLY TO MY OWN LIFE?

Esther

Esther

ESTHER 1-10

There is something everyone loves about a story of royalty, and a story of an orphan girl becoming a queen is one that seems to captivate the little girl in all of us. The book of Esther tells us about this young Jewish girl, Hadassah, known by her Persian name Esther, who would rise in rank from orphan girl to queen to deliverer of her people.

The story starts with the story of another queen, Vashti. Vashti was the queen and wife of Ahasuerus. She refused to come out during his party. Her act of defiance to the king would cause her to lose her place as queen and be banished from the palace. The king was now on the search for a new queen, and all of the kingdom's eligible young women were in the running. It is here that we are introduced to Esther as she is brought as one of the women with the potential to be queen. She goes through months of preparation until her chance with the king comes, and when her turn comes, we are told that the king loved her more than all other women. She was certainly a beautiful and virtuous woman, but we also can be assured that God was providentially working in this situation for her to become queen (Proverbs 21:1).

In the meantime, Esther's uncle Mordecai uncovered a plot to kill the king and saved his life. However, he would not bow to Haman, and this would cause some issues. Haman is hatching an evil plot to kill God's people, and Mordecai knows that Esther may be the answer to this devastating problem. Mordecai knew that because of God's covenant with His people, the Jews would be saved, but he didn't want Esther to miss the chance to be used of God. He urges her to go to the king and implores her that perhaps she has been placed in her role as queen for such a time as this. Going before the king may seem like a simple request, but in this culture it could have meant certain death for Esther. The queen was not permitted to go to the king unless he had called her, and it had been over 30 days since he had called for her.

Esther chose to go anyway, and in Esther 4:16 she tells Mordecai that if she perishes, she perishes. We have already seen what happened when Vashti defied the king, and Esther was certain that her fate would likely be far worse. But in the king's love for Esther and God's divine providence, Esther won the favor of the king and he held out his golden scepter to her. Her request was simply that the king and Haman come to dinner that she would prepare for them. When the king couldn't sleep that night, he was reminded of how Mordecai had saved his life and realized that Mordecai was never honored for his help. The king asked Haman what he should do for a man that he wanted to honor. The selfish and prideful Haman is sure that the king is speaking about him and gives his elaborate plan for his own honor, only to be told to carry it out for Mordecai.

Esther would reveal Haman's evil plot at their second dinner and plead for her own life and the life of her people. The king was disgusted by Haman's evil plan, and he hung Haman on the gallows which he had made for Mordecai. Esther had bravely and courageously saved her people. God used her because she was willing to be used. He had placed her in her exact position "for such a time as this."

God always comes through for His people. He will do what He has promised that He will do, and He will keep His covenant. We have the privilege of being used by Him in His divine plan. We can be used by the Lord, or we can let Him pass us by and use someone else. But, at the end of our lives let's look back and be able to say that we were willing servants that He used freely. He has put us in our places for such a time as this, and we want to be used in His service. His plan may not always be the easy one, but it will always be worth it to be used by the King.

"at the end of our lives let's look back and be able to say that we were willing servants that He used freely."

WHAT DO WE LEARN ABOUT GOD AND HIS CHARACTER IN THE LIFE OF ESTHER?

WHAT CHARACTER QUALITIES, POSITIVE OR NEGATIVE, DO WE SEE DEMONSTRATED IN ESTHER'S LIFE?

WHAT CAN I LEARN FROM ESTHER'S STORY THAT I CAN APPLY TO MY OWN LIFE?

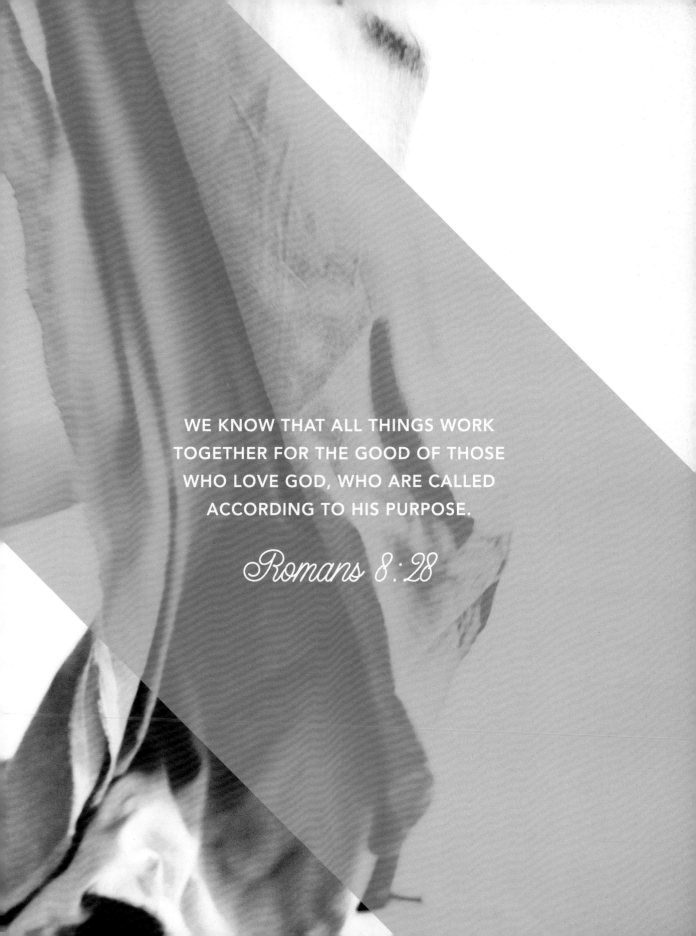

WE KNOW THAT ALL THINGS WORK
TOGETHER FOR THE GOOD OF THOSE
WHO LOVE GOD, WHO ARE CALLED
ACCORDING TO HIS PURPOSE.

Romans 8:28

WHICH WOMAN STUCK OUT TO YOU MOST THIS WEEK AND WHY?

WHAT DID YOU OBSERVE FROM THIS WEEK'S READING ABOUT GOD AND HIS CHARACTER?

WHAT DOES THIS WEEK'S READING TEACH ABOUT THE CONDITION OF MANKIND AND ABOUT YOURSELF?

HOW DOES THIS WEEK'S READING POINT TO THE GOSPEL?

HOW SHOULD YOU RESPOND TO THIS WEEK'S READING?
WHAT IS THE PERSONAL APPLICATION?

WHAT SPECIFIC ACTION STEPS CAN YOU TAKE
TO APPLY THIS WEEK'S READING?

WEEK FOUR

DAY ONE

Gomer

Gomer
HOSEA 1-14

The story of Hosea and Gomer is not your typical love story. It is a heartbreaking tale that reminds us of the steadfast and faithful love of our God even when we do not deserve it. Hosea was a prophet given a difficult task. He was commanded to marry a woman who was a prostitute to demonstrate God's incredible, faithful love to his people. The entire book of Hosea will point us to the gospel. It reminds us that although we were far from God and unlovable, His steadfast love faithfully pursued us and sought to bring us back to Himself. Gomer is the unfaithful wife and a picture of us. Her heart is prone to wander, and she is often unfaithful. And yet her husband Hosea faithfully pictures our Redeemer who is tender, gentle, and always seeking to woo her back.

In the midst of Gomer's unfaithfulness to Hosea, Hosea does something that is a perfect picture foreshadowing what Christ has done for us. Gomer left Hosea for a season, and eventually she was being sold on the market, likely as a concubine. Hosea not only loves her while she is still in her sin, but he goes and buys her back. Hosea's love was so strong that he was willing to go and buy her back even though she had been unfaithful. What a beautiful reminder that we have also been bought with a price (I Corinthians 6:20). We have been redeemed with the price of the life of our precious Savior who loved us while we were yet sinners (Romans 5:8).

The story of Hosea and Gomer reminds us that sin never satisfies—only Jesus does. It reminds us that no matter what we have done or what we will do, God is right there waiting. He is seeking to draw us back to Himself and pleading with us to return to Him. He is loving us with a steadfast love that never fails. His love is greater than our sin. And after all of our unfaithfulness to Him, He waits with open arms, ready to welcome us home.

We don't want to identify with Gomer. She doesn't have the role of the gracious heroine seen in some of the other women that we have studied; and yet, it is in her imperfection that we are reminded of our own need of the gracious love of our Savior. How often we sin and push away from Him; and yet, every single time He is there waiting to redeem and bring us back to Himself.

"no matter what we have done or what we will do, God is right there waiting."

WHAT DO WE LEARN ABOUT GOD AND HIS CHARACTER IN THE LIFE OF GOMER?

WHAT CHARACTER QUALITIES, POSITIVE OR NEGATIVE, DO WE SEE DEMONSTRATED IN GOMER'S LIFE?

WHAT CAN I LEARN FROM GOMER'S STORY THAT I CAN APPLY TO MY OWN LIFE?

Elizabeth

Elizabeth
LUKE 1:5-80

It is at the beginning of the Gospel of Luke that we are introduced to Elizabeth, and yet she was a part of God's plan for generations before. We meet her and her husband Zechariah, and we are told that they were both righteous and walked blamelessly before the Lord. In a time when many had turned their hearts from the Lord, this couple was steadfast. They were right where God had placed them, following His commandments and living righteous lives. But they had no child. Their life was full of good gifts from the Lord, and yet they must have wondered why God had never given them a child. But that was about to change.

Elizabeth's husband, Zechariah, was a priest, and he was chosen by lot to enter the temple and burn incense. It was a once in a lifetime honor, and it would turn into a day that he would never forget. The priest was to offer the incense and pray for the nation and the Messiah to come, but it seems that Zechariah had a prayer of his own that was weighing on his heart that day. It was the kind of prayer that almost seemed impossible—a prayer for a son of his own. As a priest, he would have been familiar with the stories of Abraham and Sarah, Isaac and Rebekah, and of the prayer of Hannah—and this impossible prayer was heard that day. I certainly don't think that he was expecting the answer that he received. An angel of the Lord appeared to him stating that his prayer had been heard and his wife would bear a son. Zechariah had doubts, and Gabriel said that he would not speak until it all came to pass.

God did what He said He would do, and Elizabeth conceived. Mary would come and visit Elizabeth during her pregnancy, and Elizabeth would exclaim that the child in her womb leapt for joy at the sight of her. Even the baby in her womb could recognize the presence of the Messiah.

Elizabeth would have her son, and when the time came to choose a name, she named him John just as the angel had commanded. Zechariah regains his speech as he confirmed what seemed to everyone to be an odd choice for a name. When his lips were opened, out poured praise for all God had done and for who He was. It was certainly the song of Elizabeth's heart as well. They had lived their whole lives serving the Lord, and now they had been given their heart's desire.

Isn't it just like the Lord to work like this? He took this longing couple and gave them not only a son, but a son that would prepare the way for the Messiah. We don't know if they lived long enough to see the fulfillment of this promise from the Lord, but we know that they knew their God had been faithful to them and to His people.

Our lives are often the same way. We are called to love the Lord and be faithful to Him now. We may not understand everything that He is doing, but we can know that He is faithful. He will be faithful to us. Even when we don't understand His plan, we can trust Him.

WHAT DO WE LEARN ABOUT GOD AND HIS CHARACTER IN THE LIFE OF ELIZABETH?

WHAT CHARACTER QUALITIES, POSITIVE OR NEGATIVE, DO WE SEE DEMONSTRATED IN ELIZABETH'S LIFE?

WHAT CAN I LEARN FROM ELIZABETH'S STORY THAT I CAN APPLY TO MY OWN LIFE?

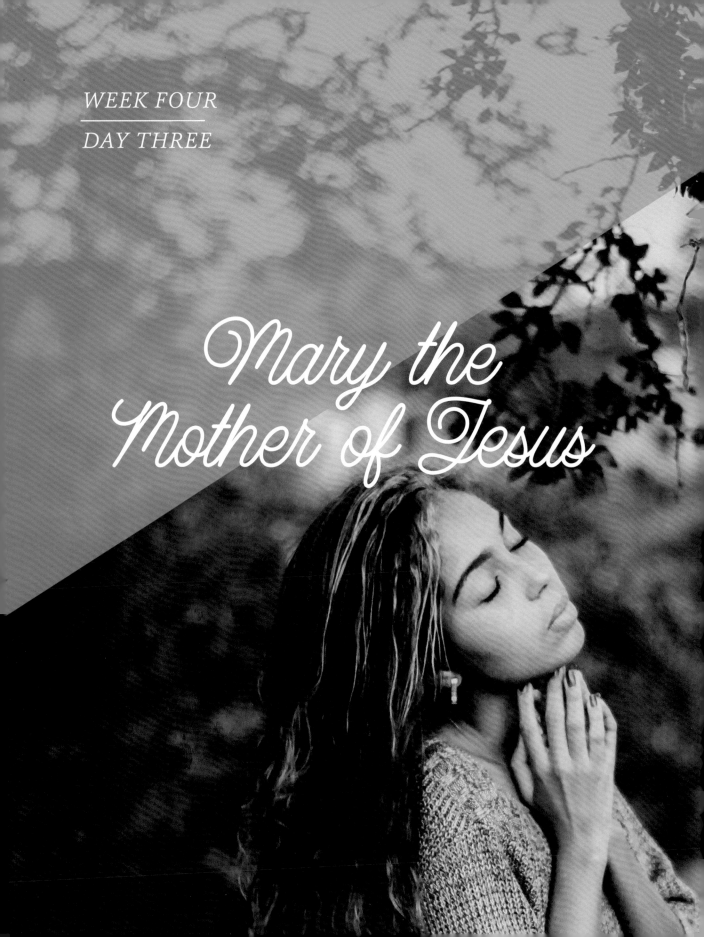

Mary the Mother of Jesus

Mary the Mother of Jesus

MATTHEW 1:18-25; 2;
LUKE 1:26-80; 2:1-52; JOHN 19:25-27

There is perhaps no woman in Scripture more well-known and highly revered than Mary. Mary, who was just a young girl when she was so blessed by the Lord, stands out as a woman greatly favored and blessed by God with the privilege of birthing the promised and long-awaited Messiah. Though Mary was certainly blessed beyond belief, some have taken it too far and have even worshiped her. Though Mary was chosen by God to fulfill a great role, she was never anything other than a finite woman. She was in need of the same grace that we are, and though Jesus was her son, He was also her Savior.

When we are introduced to Mary, she is just a young woman, likely a young teenager, who is betrothed to a man named Joseph. She came from a humble town but was a descendant of King David. She was just a young girl who may have gone unnoticed if it were not for the message that the angel brought that day. As a young Jewish girl, she would play a key role in an event that her people had been waiting centuries for. From as far back as Genesis 3, mankind had been waiting for the Messiah to come through a woman—and Mary was that woman.

Scripture is explicit that Mary was a virgin when Jesus was miraculously conceived in her womb. An unwed mother in this culture was seen as a very shameful thing, and Mary would be viewed no differently. When the angel announced to her that she was with child, she must have felt confused and perplexed. And yet her reaction is simple faith. This young girl surely knew that this event would cause scandal, and yet she submitted herself in joyful obedience. The privilege of being the mother of the promised Redeemer was far greater than any shame that would be placed on her.

We receive a precious glimpse into the heart of Mary in her song of praise. It was written after she had visited her cousin Elizabeth, who was also carrying a very special son. Her song of jubilant praise is referred to as Mary's Magnificat. In this psalm of praise, Mary not only shows her deep love for the Lord, but also her love and knowledge of God's Word. The song is full of references to dozens of passages in the Old Testament. Her praise is full of humble adoration that God would choose her to carry out this great honor.

We continue to see Mary throughout the life and ministry of Jesus, and even on the day of His crucifixion. Jesus clearly had a deep love for Mary as He entrusted her to the care of John, the beloved disciple (John 19:26-27). In some ways, she must have known that the day would come that He would die; and yet, there could not have been anything more agonizing than watching her Son die for the sins of the world and for her sin as well.

Mary's life stands as a testament to the grace found in Jesus. She was a faithful and humble woman who was chosen to be the mother of the Messiah. She would birth Him, nurture Him, raise Him, and eventually watch Him do what He had come to do. She was a woman who loved her Son and Savior and loved God's Word. Her life reminds us that God uses ordinary people who will submit to Him to do incredible things.

"Mary's life stands as a testament
to the grace found in Jesus.
She was a faithful and humble
woman who was chosen to be
the mother of the Messiah."

WHAT DO WE LEARN ABOUT GOD
AND HIS CHARACTER IN THE LIFE
OF MARY THE MOTHER OF JESUS?

WHAT CHARACTER QUALITIES,
POSITIVE OR NEGATIVE, DO WE
SEE DEMONSTRATED IN THE LIFE
OF MARY THE MOTHER OF JESUS?

WHAT CAN I LEARN FROM THE STORY
OF MARY THE MOTHER OF JESUS THAT
I CAN APPLY TO MY OWN LIFE?

WEEK FOUR
DAY FOUR

Anna

Anna
LUKE 2:22-38

Anna's whole story is recorded in three short verses in the book of Luke; and yet, those three verses give an incredible amount of insight into her life and the kind of woman that she was. With her story recorded in only three verses, it would be easy to skim past it and miss the lessons that can be learned from this faithful woman who was rewarded greatly for her faith.

Anna's story takes place just days after the birth of Jesus; and yet, her story had started so many years before. By the time we meet her, she is already 84 years old. From the information that we have, we can see that she was widowed at a very young age. Her husband had died just seven years after they were married, and she had been a widow ever since. From what the verses tell us, it is likely that she even lived on the temple grounds. People at the temple knew who she was. The Scripture calls her a prophetess. This does not mean that she was predicting the future, but instead that she was proclaiming and declaring the Word of God. Though more details are not given, it is likely that she was at the temple teaching the other women about Scripture.

Anna knew and loved God's Word. She spent her days proclaiming the truth of Scripture and praying in the temple. Though her prayers may have included many things, there is one thing that would have been at the front of her lips as she prayed in the temple day after day. She would be praying for the Messiah to come. The people were waiting anxiously for the promised Messiah. Unfortunately, when Jesus came, most did not recognize Him as the Messiah because He wasn't what they expected. But Anna was different. While praying in the temple that day, she overheard a conversation between Mary and Joseph and the priest Simeon. In that moment, the Lord opened her eyes to what was right in front of her, and she knew that this tiny baby, Jesus, was the promised Messiah.

That day, God answered the prayer that she had been praying for decades and allowed a little old lady to see the one that would change the world. He was the one she had been waiting and praying for, and she couldn't help but praise the Lord when she finally saw Him in front of her. Scripture tells us that she immediately gave thanks and then began to speak of Him to all who were waiting for redemption. The word here that tells us that she spoke implies that she not only spoke but could not stop speaking of Him. Nothing could keep her quiet after she had met Jesus. Her life had been dedicated to proclaiming the coming of the Messiah, and now she knew Him.

We can learn many things from the life of Anna. Faithfulness is the word that first comes to mind. The faithfulness of Anna is something we should certainly admire. She dedicated her life to the Lord and served Him joyfully. But most of all, we must see the faithfulness of the Lord. He heard her prayers as she prayed day after day for decades, waiting for the promised Messiah — and at just the right moment, He rewarded her for her faithfulness by showing His own. Decade after decade, He had heard every prayer of His people for the Messiah and even the prayers of this widow woman. He heard and He answered.

WHAT DO WE LEARN ABOUT GOD AND HIS CHARACTER IN THE LIFE OF ANNA?

WHAT CHARACTER QUALITIES, POSITIVE OR NEGATIVE, DO WE SEE DEMONSTRATED IN ANNA'S LIFE?

WHAT CAN I LEARN FROM ANNA'S STORY THAT I CAN APPLY TO MY OWN LIFE?

The Woman of Samaria

The Woman of Samaria

JOHN 4:1-42

We don't know her name, and yet her story is one of the most well-known in all of Scripture. The Samaritan woman, or the woman at the well, is a woman whose life is marked by sin and shame. But that all changes when she meets Jesus. Her story is our story as well. It is a story of a woman, who was an outcast, becoming a daughter of the King. It is a story of radical grace and mercy.

When Jesus is on His way to Galilee, John 4:4 tells us that He had to pass through Samaria. It is true that going through Samaria was the direct route to Galilee, but most Jews would not have taken this route. The Samaritans were seen as outsiders, and the Jews wanted nothing to do with them. Jesus had to go through Samaria that day because He had an appointment at the well of Jacob. Jesus arrived at the well around noon. Though drawing water was something that women did each day, it would never be done in the middle of the day because of the heat of the sun. The women would instead rise early in the morning and be home before the heat of the day set in. But we see this woman come at the most unlikely time. As we learn more about her, we realize that she was coming to avoid the other women and, likely, their snide remarks and disapproving glances. This woman of Samaria had made a lot of mistakes in her life, and even at that moment, her life was full of sin and scandal. She had made a lot of mistakes, but going to the well that day was certainly not one of them.

She came to the well and to her surprise Jesus asked her for a drink. Jesus was breaking down racial and cultural barriers just by talking to this woman. Men did not talk to women, Jews did not talk to Samaritans, and Jewish men definitely did not talk to Samaritan women. The woman at the well would soon learn that the man at the well was much more than just a man.

When He asked for water, she questioned Him. Why would a Jew ask for water from a Samaritan? But for every question she asked, He spoke deeper words to her. He had asked for water but then told her that she should ask Him for living water. She was confused. He had nothing to draw water with. Where would this living water come from? His words became more intriguing. He spoke of living water that gave eternal life and water that would make one never thirst again. She asked him to give her the water so she would never have to draw water again. She likely asked this because the trips to the well were full of shame for this sinful woman. He answered back, and when He asked her to call her husband, her heart sank. He was not surprised when she said that she had no husband. He told her that He knew that she didn't have a husband, but that she had previously had five and that the man she was with was not her husband. Her answer is verse 19 is almost comical as she says, "Sir, I perceive that you are a prophet." She tried to change the topic for a moment, and Jesus reminded her of the coming Messiah. God was working on this woman's heart when she said that she knew the Messiah was coming, and He would tell all things. She was realizing that she was speaking to the Messiah and that He had told her all things about herself (John 4:39). Jesus plainly told her that He was that promised Messiah.

She had come as an outcast, but there are no outcasts to Jesus. She believed on Him that day and quickly went to tell every person she could find. The woman who had come to the well at noon to avoid the people of her city now ran to them to tell them that she had found the Messiah. Jesus had taken away her shame. He took her shame and gave her a boldness that could not be explained.

She became the first evangelist to the Samaritans, as many believed in Jesus because of the word of her testimony. Her testimony pointed others to Jesus, and they saw Him for themselves, and every one that came to Him was changed forever.

We can learn a lot from this story. We are reminded that we too were sinners and outcasts who have been accepted and redeemed by Jesus. He has poured out grace and mercy on us that we did not deserve. He has taken us from outcasts to daughters. He has taken away our shame. And now we can boldly proclaim who He is because of all that He has done for us.

"Her testimony pointed others to Jesus,
and they saw Him for themselves,
and every one that came to Him
was changed forever."

"we can boldly proclaim who
He is because of all that
He has done for us."

WHAT DO WE LEARN ABOUT GOD
AND HIS CHARACTER IN THE LIFE OF
THE WOMAN OF SAMARIA?

WHAT CHARACTER QUALITIES,
POSITIVE OR NEGATIVE, DO WE SEE
DEMONSTRATED IN THE LIFE OF
THE WOMAN OF SAMARIA?

WHAT CAN I LEARN FROM THE STORY
OF THE WOMAN OF SAMARIA THAT
I CAN APPLY TO MY OWN LIFE?

"I AM THE BREAD OF LIFE," JESUS TOLD THEM. "NO ONE WHO COMES TO ME WILL EVER BE HUNGRY, AND NO ONE WHO BELIEVES IN ME WILL EVER BE THIRSTY AGAIN.

John 6:35

WHICH WOMAN STUCK OUT TO YOU MOST THIS WEEK AND WHY?

WHAT DID YOU OBSERVE FROM THIS WEEK'S READING
ABOUT GOD AND HIS CHARACTER?

WHAT DOES THIS WEEK'S READING TEACH ABOUT THE
CONDITION OF MANKIND AND ABOUT YOURSELF?

HOW DOES THIS WEEK'S READING POINT TO THE GOSPEL?

HOW SHOULD YOU RESPOND TO THIS WEEK'S READING?
WHAT IS THE PERSONAL APPLICATION?

WHAT SPECIFIC ACTION STEPS CAN YOU TAKE
TO APPLY THIS WEEK'S READING?

The Sinful Woman

The Sinful Woman

LUKE 7:36-49

Jesus is dining in the home of a prestigious Pharisee, surrounded by dinner guests, when it seems, out of nowhere, a woman enters the home. She is described as a woman of the city and as a sinner. This was certainly not the crowd that this woman was usually hanging around. She came into the house and found Him, and with no hesitation, she brought her alabaster box of ointment. Before she could even begin anointing His feet with the ointment, her tears had already anointed Him. She wept and wiped His feet with her tears and then kissed His feet and anointed Him with the precious ointment.

In that moment, the rest of the dinner party certainly was looking on with confusion at the scene before them. The Pharisee, who was hosting the party, kept silent and merely said some things to himself. But Jesus knows even the thoughts of our hearts. The Pharisee did not understand how Jesus could allow this sinful woman to touch Him. Could He even be a prophet if He allowed such things to happen? Jesus began to tell him a story about two debtors. One owed a little and one owed a lot, but neither could pay their debt. So the moneylender forgave them both. Jesus asked which one would be more grateful and love the moneylender more. Simon responded that it would be the one forgiven more, and Jesus quickly pointed out that this woman had been forgiven much and now loved much. Jesus turned to the woman and told her that her sins were forgiven and her faith had saved her.

We can learn a lot from this woman. She was desperate to get to Jesus and did whatever she had to get to Him. She had lived a life of sin and everyone knew it, but her heart was overwhelmed with love for the one man that could change everything for her. She gave Him everything she had, and she poured out her heart and her tears before Him that day. Her love for Him was obvious, but it was His love that would reach down to her that day and save her. She placed her faith in His saving grace, and she was able to go in peace.

Just like this woman, we have been saved from a great debt of sin. And now we should be desperate to get to Jesus and eager to pour out our worship to the one that we love—the one that has changed everything for us with His love and forgiveness. We love Him greatly because we have been forgiven greatly.

WHAT DO WE LEARN ABOUT GOD AND HIS CHARACTER IN THE LIFE OF THE SINFUL WOMAN?

WHAT CHARACTER QUALITIES, POSITIVE OR NEGATIVE, DO WE SEE DEMONSTRATED IN THE LIFE OF THE SINFUL WOMAN?

WHAT CAN I LEARN FROM THE SINFUL WOMAN'S STORY THAT I CAN APPLY TO MY OWN LIFE?

The Woman with the Issue of Blood

The Woman with the Issue of Blood

MATTHEW 9:20-22, MARK 5:25-34, LUKE 8:43-48

The crowd was waiting for Jesus and so was this woman. Jesus was on His way to heal a young girl, but the woman knew that He was her only hope. She had been sick for years. In the last 12 years, she had spent every penny she had on doctors that could not help her. Her disease had left her feeling like an outcast and viewed as unclean. She had heard of Jesus, and somehow she just knew that He was the one that could rescue her — she was right.

The people were pressing up against Jesus; and yet, when she reached out her hand for just a small touch of His garment, He knew. She probably thought that she could go unnoticed in such a great crowd, but no one goes unnoticed in the presence of Jesus. And with one simple touch, she knew that she had been healed. Jesus had changed everything for her. When Jesus asked who had touched Him, no one stepped forward. Dozens of people had touched Him as the crowd pressed in, and the disciples seem to chuckle at the idea that one would be singled out. She somehow realized though that He was well aware of what had just taken place, so she came forward. She proclaimed the truth that Jesus already knew: He had healed her. With just the touch of His garment, she was made clean.

He looked at her and called her "daughter" and told her that her faith had made her well. The woman who had been unclean was transformed by one simple touch. Her uncleanness could not defile Him, but His holiness had made her clean and new. One touch and everything had changed.

The same is true in our lives. One touch of the hem of His garment is enough to change everything. She was desperate to get to Jesus because she knew the power that He had. And yet in the moment that she was made clean, she was still amazed by His overwhelming grace and mercy to an outcast woman. It was not simply that she had great faith, but that she had great faith in a great God. His power to heal her transformed everything, and the tenderness of His voice was something that she would never forget. May it be something that we never forget as well. His grace toward us is overwhelming. We have been rescued to praise Him.

WHAT DO WE LEARN ABOUT GOD
AND HIS CHARACTER IN THE LIFE OF THE
WOMAN WITH THE ISSUE OF BLOOD?

WHAT CHARACTER QUALITIES,
POSITIVE OR NEGATIVE, DO WE SEE
DEMONSTRATED IN THE LIFE OF THE
WOMAN WITH THE ISSUE OF BLOOD?

WHAT CAN I LEARN FROM THE STORY OF
THE WOMAN WITH THE ISSUE OF BLOOD
THAT I CAN APPLY TO MY OWN LIFE?

Martha

Martha

LUKE 10:38-42; JOHN 11:1-12:3

In so many ways most women can identify with Martha. She was a level-headed woman who is seen in Scripture taking care of her family and taking care of others. She was a doer. She was a woman of hospitality. She made things happen. And yet somehow, in all of her doing, the Savior needed to remind her to be still and to choose Him. Jesus reminded her that even though her serving was noble, honorable, and good, there was something better — sitting at His feet.

We meet Martha as she is welcoming Jesus into her home. We can learn from other passages of Scripture that it seems Martha and her siblings, Mary and Lazarus, had a very close relationship with Jesus. The Lord speaks tenderly to them, and in later passages we will learn that He loved them very dearly. On this particular instance, as Martha is welcoming Jesus into her home, we learn that her sister Mary was sitting at Jesus' feet. Martha was distracted however. As a hostess, she couldn't have had a more important guest, and I can only imagine that she wanted things to be perfect for Him. While her sister sat and listened to Jesus, Martha rushed through the house doing all of the things that needed to be done — all of the things that would make this the perfect experience for Jesus. Soon her frustration with her sister boiled over, and she went and rebuked her in front of Jesus. She must have thought that certainly Jesus would see her plight and make Mary come and help her. I can imagine that her heart changed the moment He said her name. His tender and loving words reminded her of her own heart. He had seen her all along. She was anxious, busy, and concerned about everything but the one thing that was most important. She was doing good things, but not the best thing. He reminded her that Mary had, in fact, chosen the better thing. Sitting at Jesus' feet is always better.

The next time we see Martha is when her brother Lazarus died. When he was still sick, Mary and Martha had sent word to Jesus. Jesus did not come right away, but John 11:5 tells us that Jesus loved them. In our minds it seems so perplexing. Jesus loved this family; and yet, He did not come right away. He waited until it seemed too late. When Jesus arrived in the little town of Bethany, Lazarus had already been in the grave for four days. People were coming to grieve with the two sisters, but Jesus was bringing a hope that they could not imagine. Martha ran out to meet Jesus when He arrived, and likely with tears in her eyes, she told Him that she knew that if He had been there, Lazarus would not have died. It didn't make sense. Why hadn't He come when He could have changed everything? Jesus spoke to her of the resurrection, but her mind could only comprehend that He must be talking about the future. But Jesus performed a miracle there that day, and Lazarus walked out of the tomb.

Martha reminds us of so many things. We are so often prone to make the same mistakes that she did; and yet, just like she was, we are greatly loved by our Savior. Her life and testimony remind us that Jesus is more concerned with us sitting at His feet than doing great things for Him. We must be careful not to do so much for the Lord that we neglect to be with the Lord and to take time to know Him. He would rather have our hearts and our worship than service. We must be careful to not focus so much on our good works that we lose focus of our precious Savior. Martha was a woman who greatly loved the Lord and who was greatly loved by the Lord, but her priorities slipped out of place. She shifted her gaze from Jesus to all that needed to be done, and the result was an overwhelmed heart and anxious spirit. It can easily happen to us as well. These are always the results when we take our eyes off of Jesus and put them on all of the things that so easily distract us from who He is. Making Jesus our first choice and top priority is something that we must choose each and every day. It doesn't just happen. But the more time we spend at His feet, the more our hearts will desire and delight in being with Him. When He becomes everything to us, everything else will fall into place. We will find peace and contentment at the feet of Jesus no matter what circumstances we face. And little by little He will grow our faith and make us more like Himself.

"Making Jesus our first choice and top priority is something that we must choose each and every day. It doesn't just happen. But the more time we spend at His feet, the more our hearts will desire and delight in being with Him."

WHAT DO WE LEARN ABOUT GOD AND HIS CHARACTER IN THE LIFE OF MARTHA?

WHAT CHARACTER QUALITIES, POSITIVE OR NEGATIVE, DO WE SEE DEMONSTRATED IN MARTHA'S LIFE?

WHAT CAN I LEARN FROM MARTHA'S STORY THAT I CAN APPLY TO MY OWN LIFE?

Mary of Bethany

Mary of Bethany

Mary of Bethany is mentioned in all four of the Gospels, and everywhere she is mentioned she is seen as a woman who loved and served the Lord with everything she had and everything she was. Every time she is seen in Scripture she is at the feet of Jesus. She poured out not only her precious ointment but also her heart and life into the love and service of Jesus. While her sister and others were distracted by this life, her eyes were fixed on Jesus alone. She was a worshiper who loved her Savior.

In the familiar account of Mary and Martha entertaining Jesus in their home, Martha was busy serving and being the perfect hostess. Mary's eyes were so fixed on Jesus that it seems she didn't even realize how her sister rushed around trying to accomplish a million little tasks for this important dinner. Instead, Mary was found at Jesus' feet. She was soaking in every word that He said, almost oblivious to all that was happening around her. She was desperately aware of the privilege of His presence. There was nothing more important to her than time with Jesus.

Whether you identify more with Mary or with Martha, Mary reminds us that we have to choose our priorities. We can allow ourselves to become distracted by good things, or we can choose to focus on Jesus. He is the very best thing.

The next time Mary is seen in Scripture is at the death of Lazarus, her brother. Mary and Martha had called for Jesus, but from their limited perspective, He had not gotten there in time and Lazarus was now dead for four days. When Jesus did come, Mary fell at His feet and proclaimed that she knew if He had been there, her brother would not have died. She wept before Him. She did not seek to hide her heart from Him. Her heart was confused and broken, and the tears she shed were not unnoticed by her Savior. As she weeps before Him, a short verse in John 11 tells us that Jesus wept. Jesus did not weep because Lazarus had died. As the sovereign Lord, He knew what was coming next. Jesus wept because He feels the hurt of His children. He loved Mary and He saw and felt her pain. Jesus would raise Lazarus that day, and I don't think that Mary would ever get over the miracle that He did for her. She was seeing a glimpse of His great love for her that would only be proven more and more as the next days and weeks played out.

In many ways, it was the raising of Lazarus that put things over the edge. When the religious leaders heard that Jesus had raised a man from the dead, it was the final push that they needed to confirm the plan in their hearts that Jesus must be killed. In some ways, it seems that Mary knew that. The miracle performed for her family was, in so many ways, the beginning of the crucifixion narrative. Shortly after the raising of Lazarus, Jesus is again eating at the home of Mary and Martha. As they all sat at the table, Mary came in, took a pound of the most expensive ointment, anointed Jesus, and wiped His feet with her hair. She was showing her humility and breaking down cultural barriers just by loosening her hair which was seen as culturally unacceptable for a woman to do. But Mary was not concerned about her own pride or cultural barriers; she was concerned about her Savior. She wanted to worship Jesus. The woman who was always seen at Jesus' feet is now seen there again in an act of extravagant worship. She brought her alabaster box of ointment and her unyielding love and gratitude for her Savior. She was anointing Him for burial, and Jesus promised that her act of love would be remembered forever.

Mary reminds us of the kind of unashamed worship we should have for the Lord. She reminds us to be women found always at the feet of Jesus. Women who are not distracted by all the things that have to be done, but who are consumed with one thing only – Jesus. Her life is a reminder that Jesus sees us in our pain and suffering and weeps with us. Even though He is God, He sees us and sympathizes in our humanity. Though His plan is best, He knows that we cannot always see that, and He weeps with us as we experience the pain and grief that life so often brings. He sees us, and He is moved with compassion for the ones that He loves so dearly. And when we see the extravagant love of our Savior like Mary did, we will react the same way that she did — in extravagant worship. Her life was forever changed by Jesus, and she lived to know Him and worship Him more each day. May we be women who do the same. May we be women who are always found at the feet of Jesus.

"Mary reminds us of the kind of unashamed worship we should have for the Lord. She reminds us to be women found always at the feet of Jesus."

WHAT DO WE LEARN ABOUT GOD AND
HIS CHARACTER IN THE LIFE OF MARY
OF BETHANY?

WHAT CHARACTER QUALITIES, POSITIVE
OR NEGATIVE, DO WE SEE DEMONSTRAT-
ED IN MARY OF BETHANY'S LIFE?

WHAT CAN I LEARN FROM MARY OF
BETHANY'S STORY THAT I CAN APPLY
TO MY OWN LIFE?

The Widow with Two Coins

The Widow with Two Coins

MARK 12:41-44; LUKE 21:1-4

We don't know her name, but Jesus did that day when she entered the Court of the Women to put her tiny offering in the box. Her offering didn't seem like much in comparison to those that rushed around the temple that day with much larger offerings. The rich seemed to make a show that day as they dropped their great offerings into the offering box. This widow would have likely gone unnoticed by everyone that day as she dropped two small copper coins into the offering box. But Jesus saw her. Jesus noticed.

While the rich people gave much larger offerings due to their abundance, she gave everything she had. It wasn't a great sum of money and it would have been easy for her to feel like there was no point in even giving such a small offering. But her heart was pure and her love for God was sincere. It took great faith for her to put her widow's mites into the box that day. Giving her money would mean that there would be struggle, but her heart must have been filled with joy as she gave all that she had. Love and faith in God were the only things that would motivate someone to give all that they had. And that day, Jesus would see her clearly. In a steady stream of people that gave much bigger gifts, Jesus saw the woman who gave with a pure and thankful heart.

How easy it is for us to think that what we have to offer isn't as good as what others have to give. So often, it seems that others have been given greater gifts and talents and areas of service. So often, our day to day service to the Lord can seem so mundane compared to what others are doing — but Jesus sees us. He sees us serving in the simple things, and He sees our heart. He is more concerned about a heart that is totally dedicated to Him than He is about great gifts of money or service. He wants our hearts. He wants women with hearts that are fully dedicated to Him. God's economy is different than ours, and He is much more concerned with our hearts than with the magnitude of our gifts. Your service is not unnoticed by the King of Kings. He sees you serving in the simple things, and He is pleased. He sees us right where we are, and even our most humble offerings become a symphony of praise to our Savior when they are given from a heart of love for our God.

"He is much more concerned with our hearts than with the magnitude of our gifts."

"He sees us right where we are, and even our most humble offerings become a symphony of praise to our Savior when they are given from a heart of love for our God."

WHAT DO WE LEARN ABOUT GOD
AND HIS CHARACTER IN THE LIFE OF
THE WIDOW WITH TWO COINS?

WHAT CHARACTER QUALITIES,
POSITIVE OR NEGATIVE, DO WE
SEE DEMONSTRATED IN THE LIFE
OF THE WIDOW WITH TWO COINS?

WHAT CAN I LEARN FROM THE STORY
OF THE WIDOW WITH TWO COINS
THAT I CAN APPLY TO MY OWN LIFE?

CASTING ALL YOUR CARES ON HIM,
BECAUSE HE CARES ABOUT YOU.

1 Peter 5:7

WEEK FIVE

reflection

WHICH WOMAN STUCK OUT TO YOU MOST THIS WEEK AND WHY?

WHAT DID YOU OBSERVE FROM THIS WEEK'S READING ABOUT GOD AND HIS CHARACTER?

WHAT DOES THIS WEEK'S READING TEACH ABOUT THE CONDITION OF MANKIND AND ABOUT YOURSELF?

HOW DOES THIS WEEK'S READING POINT TO THE GOSPEL?

HOW SHOULD YOU RESPOND TO THIS WEEK'S READING?
WHAT IS THE PERSONAL APPLICATION?

WHAT SPECIFIC ACTION STEPS CAN YOU TAKE
TO APPLY THIS WEEK'S READING?

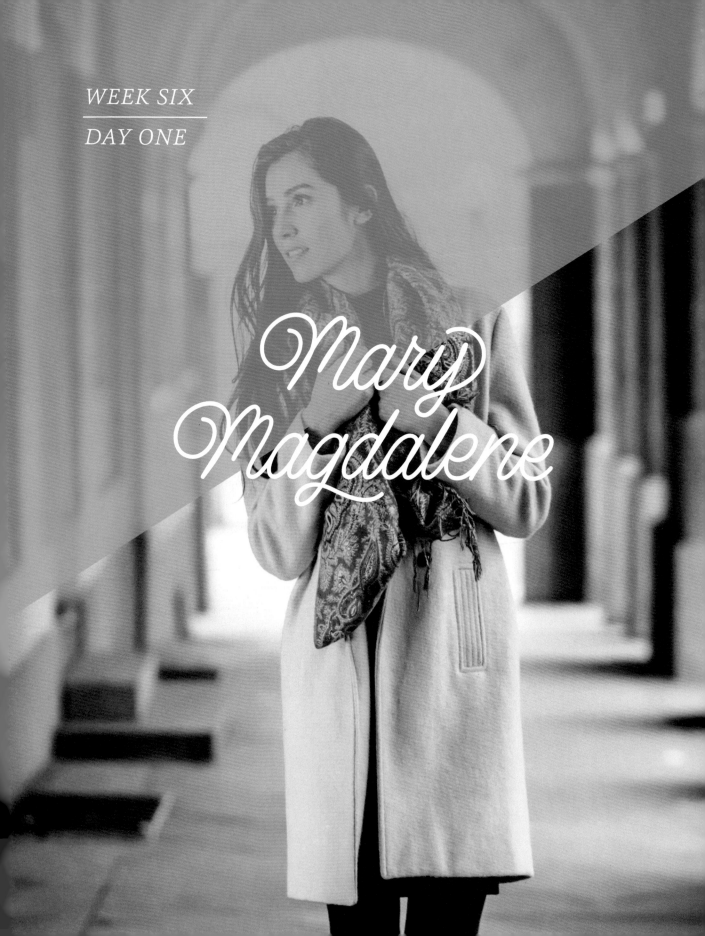

Mary Magdalene

Mary Magdalene

MATTHEW 27:55-61; 28:1-10; MARK 15-16;
LUKE 8:1-3; 24:1-12; JOHN 19:25; 20:1-18

Mary Magdalene is one of the most prominent women in the New Testament. She is mentioned by name in all four Gospels and was the first person that Jesus revealed Himself to after the resurrection.

From these distinctions, it might seem as if she was an important and affluent woman, but her life had once been full of darkness before she met Jesus. However, she clung to Jesus because He delivered her. She knew that she owed Him everything. In Luke 8:1-3 we learn that Jesus had cast seven demons out of her, and now she traveled with Jesus and the disciples. Her life had been radically transformed after meeting Jesus. She had lived a life of darkness and oppression. When she finally glimpsed Jesus, she knew that she had seen the true Light, and nothing would ever be the same for her again.

She is mentioned by name in every one of the four Gospels, but the thing she is most well-known for is coming to the tomb the morning of the resurrection. Scripture tells us that she had been there during the crucifixion. She had looked on with Jesus' mother as her whole world came crumbling down. After all Jesus had done for her, she would have done everything to rescue Him that day. I wonder if she fully knew how He was rescuing her that day. She looked on and wept as she watched her Savior and her friend die on that dark day. When Joseph and Nicodemus placed Him in the tomb, she watched carefully. When Sunday came, she went to the tomb with the finest spices to anoint His body properly. After all that He had done for her, it must have felt like the only thing she could do to rise early that morning and properly anoint and prepare His body. The scenes of that crucifixion afternoon and all her time with Jesus must have raced through her mind as she walked to the tomb that morning. The women wondered how they would be able to move the heavy stone, but when they arrived they found that the stone had already been moved — and the tomb was empty.

It seems the rest of the women and disciples scattered, but Mary stood there in the garden weeping. She lifted her gaze to the empty tomb as the tears filled her eyes. Then, as she turned around toward the garden, a man stood in her midst. She did not recognize Him when He asked her why she was weeping and who she was seeking. With one word, everything changed: "Mary." He said her name and a rush of emotion came over her. She knew it was Jesus. He called her by name, and she knew His tender voice (John 10:3-4).

She didn't know that she would be the first to witness the resurrection that morning, but she knew that Jesus had changed everything for her and she would pour out her love in any way possible. It is significant that Jesus appeared first to a woman, let alone a woman with a past. To others, she may not have been the most credible witness, but Jesus knew that a woman that had been redeemed by His mercy and grace was just the type of person to proclaim His resurrection.

Mary's life reminds us that God uses people from every walk of life. He uses women that have felt pain and sorrow, women that have been raised in the ways of the Lord, and women who have been redeemed from darkness. He uses women who are courageous enough to follow Jesus no matter what. He uses women who have tasted His goodness and seen the power of His love. He uses women like you and me.

"He uses women who are courageous enough to follow Jesus no matter what. He uses women who have tasted His goodness and seen the power of His love."

WHAT DO WE LEARN ABOUT GOD
AND HIS CHARACTER IN THE LIFE
OF MARY MAGDALENE?

WHAT CHARACTER QUALITIES, POSITIVE OR
NEGATIVE, DO WE SEE DEMONSTRATED IN
MARY MAGDALENE'S LIFE?

WHAT CAN I LEARN FROM MARY
MAGDALENE'S STORY THAT I CAN
APPLY TO MY OWN LIFE?

Lydia

Lydia

ACTS 16:6-40

We encounter Lydia in the book of Acts as the gospel begins to spread throughout the world. She has the unique distinction of being the very first convert in Europe. As Timothy, Paul, and Silas travel preaching the gospel, Paul is urged by the Lord in a dream to go to Philippi in Macedonia, which was located in modern day Greece. Jewish tradition at the time dictated that there needed to be ten Jewish men for a synagogue to be formed, and Phillipi did not even have this small number. With no synagogue to preach in, they went and preached to the women where they prayed. It was there that Lydia, who was a Gentile business woman, heard the gospel. Her heart was opened by the Lord to the beautiful message of redemption that Paul preached that day. Her heart was captured by the God of the gospel and the grace that is found in Jesus, and she believed and was baptized along with her entire house that day.

Lydia did what she could. She opened her home and her heart to Paul and Silas and showed great hospitality. When Paul and Silas were arrested and eventually released from jail, it was to Lydia's home that they went. It was there that they found her hospitality once again as well as the encouragement they needed to carry on and continue spreading the gospel throughout Europe. Lydia was not afraid to be identified with Paul and Silas and ultimately with Jesus, and her simple hospitality and encouragement greatly contributed to the spread of the gospel in Europe and through the whole world.

How easy it is to think that we do not have much to offer. Yet, when we do what we can and use the gifts that God has given us, we may never know the ways that our life will impact others and help spread the gospel. Each of us has been given unique gifts and abilities that we can use to serve others, and, ultimately, to serve the Lord. Lydia had been blessed as a business woman, and she used the home that she had been blessed with to entertain the ones that would preach the gospel. She offered encouragement and hospitality and did what she could.

Lydia reminds us to have hearts that are open and ready to hear from the Lord, and quick to act in faithfulness and service to Him. Her life teaches us to use what we have been given for Him. No gift or offering is too small when it is given to Jesus. He will take whatever we have to offer Him and use it for our good and for His glory, and Lydia's life is a testament to that truth.

WHAT DO WE LEARN ABOUT GOD AND
HIS CHARACTER IN THE LIFE OF LYDIA?

WHAT CHARACTER QUALITIES, POSITIVE
OR NEGATIVE, DO WE SEE DEMONSTRATED
IN LYDIA'S LIFE?

WHAT CAN I LEARN FROM LYDIA'S STORY
THAT I CAN APPLY TO MY OWN LIFE?

WEEK SIX
—————
DAY THREE

Priscilla

Priscilla

ACTS 18-19; ROMANS 16:3-4; 1 CORINTHIANS 16:19; 2 TIMOTHY 4:19

Though we do not know a ton about Priscilla, we see her name mentioned several times throughout Scripture, and we can gather several things about her from the times that she is mentioned. She is a woman who served the Lord wherever she could. She said "yes" to the Lord and served the Lord in the small things and in the great. Because of her great faith and service to the Lord, she would have a great impact on the formation of the early church.

We meet Priscilla in Acts 18 when Paul came to stay and work with her and her husband Aquila. We see her as a woman who was industrious, working with her husband in their tent-making business. She was a woman of hospitality, as she welcomed Paul into her home so that he could do the work of the Lord in Corinth. Priscilla and Aquila went with Paul as missionaries to Syria. Priscilla was a woman of the Word, and she knew the Scriptures. Priscilla and her husband would then disciple and teach Apollos about the Lord. Apollos would continue on to minister and encourage many because of the sound doctrine and teaching he had learned from Priscilla and Aquila. The book of Romans would also tell us that Priscilla and Aquila risked their lives to save Paul, and that both Paul and the entire church were indebted to them.

Priscilla's acts of obedience may have seemed so small in the moment. Yet each step of obedience was a simple act of worship that would have a tremendous impact on the early church. From opening her home in hospitality, to going as one of the first missionaries, to teaching sound doctrine to the young Apollos who would have a great impact for the Lord, and risking her life for Paul and for the sake of the gospel, Priscilla was a woman who lived her daily life to serve the Lord and those around her.

Priscilla's life reminds us to serve the Lord every day. She reminds us that every small act of service is an act of beautiful worship and praise when it is done for the Lord from a heart of love. It may often seem to us that our small contributions to the kingdom are insignificant, but when we are where God has called us to be, there is no act of service that is insignificant to the Lord. Each small act of love and service adds up to a life that is completely devoted to the Lord and poured out for His glory.

WHAT DO WE LEARN ABOUT GOD AND HIS
CHARACTER IN THE LIFE OF PRISCILLA?

WHAT CHARACTER QUALITIES,
POSITIVE OR NEGATIVE, DO WE SEE
DEMONSTRATED IN PRISCILLA'S LIFE?

WHAT CAN I LEARN FROM PRISCILLA'S
STORY THAT I CAN APPLY TO
MY OWN LIFE?

JUST AS EACH ONE HAS RECEIVED
A GIFT, USE IT TO SERVE OTHERS,
AS GOOD STEWARDS OF THE
VARIED GRACE OF GOD.

1 Peter 4:10

reflection

WHICH WOMAN STUCK OUT TO YOU MOST THIS WEEK AND WHY?

WHAT DID YOU OBSERVE FROM THIS WEEK'S READING
ABOUT GOD AND HIS CHARACTER?

WHAT DOES THIS WEEK'S READING TEACH ABOUT THE
CONDITION OF MANKIND AND ABOUT YOURSELF?

HOW DOES THIS WEEK'S READING POINT TO THE GOSPEL?

HOW SHOULD YOU RESPOND TO THIS WEEK'S READING?
WHAT IS THE PERSONAL APPLICATION?

WHAT SPECIFIC ACTION STEPS CAN YOU TAKE
TO APPLY THIS WEEK'S READING?

What is the gospel?

Thank you for reading and enjoying this study with us! We are abundantly grateful for theWord of God, the instruction we glean from it, and the ever-growing understanding aboutGod's character from it. We're also thankful that Scripture continually points to one thing ininnumerable ways: the gospel.

We remember our brokenness when we read about the fall of Adam and Eve in the gardenof Eden (Genesis 3), when sin entered into a perfect world and maimed it. We rememberthe necessity that something innocent must die to pay for our sin when we read about theatoning sacrifices in the Old Testament. We read that we have all sinned and fallen short ofthe glory of God (Romans 3:23), and that the penalty for our brokenness, the wages of oursin, is death (Romans 6:23). We all are in need of grace, mercy, and most importantly—weall need a Savior.

We consider the goodness of God when we realize that He did not plan to leave us in thisdire state. We see His promise to buy us back from the clutches of sin and death in Genesis3:15. And we see that promise accomplished with Jesus Christ on the cross. Jesus Christ knewno sin yet became sin so that we might become righteous through His sacrifice (2 Corinthians5:21.) Jesus was tempted in every way that we are and lived sinlessly. He was reviled, yet stillyielded Himself for our sake, that we may have life abundant in Him. Jesus lived the perfectlife that we could not live, and died the death that we deserved.

The gospel is profound yet simple. There are many mysteries in it that we can never exhaustthis side of heaven, but there is still overwhelming weight to its implications in this life. Thegospel is the telling of our sinfulness and God's goodness, and this gracious gift compels aresponse. We are saved by grace through faith, (Ephesians 2:9) which means that we rest withfaith in the grace that Jesus Christ displayed on the cross. We cannot save ourselves from ourbrokenness or do any amount of good works to merit God's favor, but we can have faith thatwhat Jesus accomplished in His death, burial, and resurrection was more than enough forour salvation and our eternal delight. When we accept God, we are commanded to die to our self and our sinful desires and live a life worthy of the calling we have received (Ephesians 4:1).The gospel compels us to be sanctified, and in so doing, we are conformed to the likenessof Christ Himself.

This is hope. This is redemption. This is the gospel.

HE MADE THE ONE WHO DID
NOT KNOW SIN TO BE SIN FOR US,
SO THAT IN HIM WE MIGHT BECOME
THE RIGHTEOUSNESS OF GOD.

2 Corinthians 5:21

Thank you

FOR STUDYING GOD'S
WORD WITH US!

CONNECT WITH US:

@THEDAILYGRACECO
@KRISTINSCHMUCKER

CONTACT US:

INFO@THEDAILYGRACECO.COM

SHARE:

#THEDAILYGRACECO
#LAMPANDLIGHT

WEBSITE:

WWW.THEDAILYGRACECO.COM